just breathe

A Parent's Guide to Distance Learning:

4 Critical Steps to Setting Up Successful Virtual Learning Environments at Home

Susan Pearl-Weese, M. Ed.

FOREWARD

Help, I am drowning in a virtual world! Most of you have been thrown in at the deep end of the pool by suddenly assuming the role of teacher's helper for your children. I am here to let you know that creating an awesome Learning Environment is not as difficult as you might imagine. Teachers have been doing it for years and have faced the very same challenges that you yourself are now facing. I faced those same challenges and failed many, many times.

During my first few years of teaching, I cannot count how many times I found myself locked in the faculty restroom crying my eyes out due to one of my tough days. Children, God love 'em, are challenging! My husband has a saying that he got from his father. "One kid is a kid, two kids is half a kid". Two children are harder to manage than one, and as the numbers go up, so does the inattention and potential problems. Every parent has a managing system that we call parenting, and that works great for home life. Educational stress increases the demand on the child, parent, and teacher. Teachers have learned that it is impossible to control children, we must manage the Learning Environment.

Managing Learning Environments is a skill. And I just did not have it when I started. Veteran teachers made it look so easy. You walk into their classrooms and everyone is working, getting along, lining up in line correctly, talking respectfully, and generally completing all their work. Magic? Right!? What did those teachers have that I did not? What did they know that I did not know? I will tell you. They had TOOLS and EXPERIENCE. Once I had those TOOLS, I started getting compliments too. How quiet my class was. How busy my students were. How few office referrals I had. It only took several long, frustrating, emotionally draining, headache producing YEARS for me to get it.

Parents, today, do not have years to work on classroom management. Your children and you have needs right now that require Protocols, Procedures, and Expectations and that is what I will demonstrate to you in this short book. Take what you need, leave the rest, make it your own because every child and every family is different. What works for others might not work for you, so feel free to create something in your own style. Most of the examples, in this book, are just examples of the structure. It is the structure that is the most important element.

CONTENTS

Empowering Parents   i

1   Protocols   1

2   Procedures   6

3   Expectations   10

4   Managing Behavior   17

5   Educationally Relevant Activities   25

    Conclusion   27

    Dedication   28

    Resources   29

    About Author   30

EMPOWERING PARENTS

"I am hanging on to sanity by a thread." That is what so many parents have said to me over the past couple of years while everyone was trying distance learning for the first time. The appreciation for teachers skyrocketed while parents were juggling being mommies or daddies and the home teacher at the same time. How did it work??? Not so great for some, some gave up, some started wine clubs, some did great! Why did it seem so difficult? Because parents need to put on their teacher hat and not the parent hat. Your parent/child relationship is slightly different than the coach/child relationship. It is much like taking off one hat and putting on another. The teacher is objective. The teacher does not take things personally when a child has behaviors. The teacher does not think "Everyone is going to think I am a horrible parent." They think "this child is having a problem and I need to figure out what system will help them."

During my first year of teaching, I got nervous when veteran teachers came to observe my classes. I knew I was still working on creating a fluent learning environment and here come the teachers that can do it while standing on their head, singing the ABC song, and knitting all at the same time. Was I intimidated? Yes! Embarrassed? Yes! Envious? Absolutely! That is because veteran teachers have practiced year after year the Art of Expectations, Procedures, Protocols, and Consequences. All the elements that I was just starting to learn, create, and expand in my classroom. Did I want my class to run as smoothly as theirs? You bet! Why? Because their students learned the most and demonstrated it every day. Their students enjoyed their classes. Their students were well-behaved students. Their students loved their teacher. The student's parents loved those teachers. I wanted to be like them too. I wanted to give that opportunity to my students. I wanted to be the avenue to success for those students. I wanted to deliver an entire lesson without one interruption! Did I do all that in my first year? No! Not even close. Why? Because most of the tools are not taught in teacher prep programs, they are learned on the ground in class with children.

So, I spent the next 5 years learning about classroom management. I took classes, went to seminars, read books, watched other teachers, asked questions of other teachers, tried out strategies, learned, and planned some more. I had to re-create my Expectations several times until I found what worked for me, fit my personality, and worked with my students. I still update them from time to time as the class changes, needs change or I change. After teaching in traditional schools for 15 years, I moved over to a virtual educational program where I teach through a virtual classroom. I love it because I spend more time in small groups or one-on-one with students. I still utilize the system online, but it looks quite different in the virtual world. I also found that I spent a lot of time explaining to parents how to get their children engaged in learning online. Suddenly, I was not in charge of the Learning Environment anymore.

News Flash! Now the parents are the ones creating the Learning Environment. Each of my student's parents has assumed the role of caretaker of the Learning Environment. That is when it hit, and I realized that they did not have the same information that I had. They were struggling with the same issues that I had my first few years of teaching. How do I get my students engaged? How do I keep them on task? How do I reduce the distractions? How do I create an environment that they can be successful in? WE, *the parents, and I*, want these students to learn to their fullest potential, demonstrate what they know, and apply that information to everything that they do. It is now a partnership, a shared responsibility, to provide these students with the knowledge and skills they need to become successful adults. WOW! This is new to all of us. For years, teachers have solely held the responsibility of all aspects of educational success. Now we share that responsibility, but parents do not have the same tools that we have learned over the years. That is when I decided that I needed to start sharing the information that I learned, my experiences, my failures, my successes, and my processes in order to give parents the same opportunities for success that I had.

In this book, I have compiled the elements of what I found worked and in the order that I set them up for each class. I would like to stress that you need to start with Protocols and follow the critical steps in order. Why in that order? It seems like the behaviors pop up first and then you must deal with them. True, and you might have some distraction, arguing, negotiation, etc, pop up first, and it will take a few repetitions (10-40 depending on the child), but I can guarantee you that if you set up the Learning Environment with Protocols first and follow the sequence of Procedures and then Expectations, by the time you get to Consequences (behavior management) you won't have much behavior to manage. The first 3 steps will take care of almost all behavior concerns that you might have, and you will not need to move to the Consequence often. It is that magical!

As you read through the chapters, I will explain how to create these things, why we create these things, and what the benefit to you will be. These 4 things are ESSENTIAL to Learning Environment management and every classroom teacher on the planet probably practices these 4 elements every day. It is the difference between complete chaos and an awesome learning environment. The best part of the entire concept is that it costs almost nothing to start and maintain. And you can do it too!

1 PROTOCOLS

Why do most schools have so many bells that ring all the time? To keep us sane and on track. Protocols are a set of structured processes, processes that include scheduling, dedicated workspaces, guidelines for tasks (writing, test-taking), grading assignments, etc. Most parents are not aware of protocols because they are embedded in every school setting. Protocols are all the structure of the daily school environment. Now let's talk about how you would use protocols at home. Protocols for distance learning covers things like what time do we go to a reading group online, when is lunch, and what time is the end of the school day.

For every teacher, scheduling in the most important thing to set up first. Having a daily schedule provides structure and reliability for the school. When students know when to do things, when activities change when recess is when lunch is and when the end of the school day is, they feel more in control of their own actions and schedules which begins to create the feeling of being comfortable in the environment. Predictability is key and students rely on it. One day at school can look like an eternity to a child. Breaking the day up into sections/chunks makes the daily schedule more manageable for children. Posting a daily schedule helps, having a bell to ring at the end of each session, setting solid but accommodated time for learning can increase focus and work completion.

You might ask, how much time should it take to complete lessons. The average time is about 40 mins per subject, give or take, depending on the student's age or ability level of the student. Younger students might take longer, and high school students might have bigger projects. One important concept that teachers are aware of is that the human brain can only absorb information for about 20 minutes max. Anything longer than that will mean that some of the information gets lost. Comprehension decreases after 20 mins. Teachers break up instruction into smaller units of learning so that no student must sit and concentrate for hours at a time. In an online classroom, most lesson plans are set up for 20 minutes of direct teacher-led instruction, 5-10 minutes discussions/sharing. You will find in virtual classrooms that teachers use strategies like partner pair share, round-robin re-tell, jigsaw discussions, etc. to break up the instruction, provide a mental break and allow students to process the information by discussing it because verbally processing information can be key to retention as well.

Let us do the math, 5 subjects X 30 minutes equals roughly 2 and ½ hours of direct instruction daily. The rest of the school day in traditional schools is filled with discussion, recess, standing in lines, going to lunch, waiting for busses or bells, locker time, library time, computer time, social time, and lining up to go "somewhere" time. If some of your children are done with all their schoolwork in 3 hours, check their work and if it is 80% or better, then they are done! When you take out all the "wait" time in the average school day, most of the coursework can be completed in **3 hours or less** every day.

Suggested schedules for Distance Learning is 30-40 minutes of computer lessons (depending on age) and a 15-minute break. You can do that with all the children in the household or stagger the start times and break times if you want opportunities for one-on-one interaction. A possible schedule might look like this:

Opening - **8:00 a.m.**: Activity of your choice to get the day started (breakfast, happy thoughts, pledge, prayer, mediation, yoga, announcements, housekeeping, etc.)

1st Period - **8:30** a.m.
Reading Group: 20 mins
Task/Reflection: 15 mins
Break: 15 mins

2nd Period - **9:20 a.m.**
Math Lesson: 20 mins
Task/Reflection 15 mins
Break: 15 mins

3rd Period - **10:10 a.m.**
Science: 20 mins
Task/Reflection: 15 mins
Break: 15 mins

4th Period - **11:00 a.m.**
Social Studies: 20 mins

Task/Reflection: 15 mins
Break: 15 mins

Lunch: **11:40 - 12:30 p.m.**

5th Period - **12:30 p.m.**
Ed Tech/Art: 20 mins
Task/Reflection: 15 mins
Break: 15 mins

6th Period: **1:10 p.m.**
Elective: 20 mins
Task/Reflection: 15 mins

End of the school day: **1:45 p.m.**

This suggested schedule is a starting place for you. Younger students might need shorter periods and secondary students might need more time or less time. You might need three different schedules depending on the grade levels of your children. If you have students on multiple grade levels, then consider downloading a timer app like a bell schedule for your child's computer. The bell will ring only on the computer that it's installed on and you can set the times that you want the bell to ring so that it meets the schedule that you have built. It is a great way to have each of your children working on their own schedule. You can alternate times if you do not want some of them or all of them with the same break times. Alternating breaks will give you opportunities for one-on-one time with each of your children.

Be aware that all students work at their own pace. Some can complete all their work on a subject in 20 minutes, do not need a break, go on to the next subject, and then get done with everything earlier. What is your Protocol if one is working and the other is done? What is the Protocol in place if 6 hours is not enough for one child to get 4 subjects done? Thinking through some of these possibilities and having a solution first will save you many headaches and problems once you are in the thick of it when thinking things through is not an option. One of the most important tasks to do is to come up with a list of options that you are comfortable with having your children do. If you do not want your children consuming video games all afternoon, then do not make it one of the options. However, it is important to choose activities that your children have some interest in. Nothing is more frustrating than trying to get a child to perform a free time activity that they are not remotely interested in. So, if you want them to watch educational videos, let them choose the topic. If you want them to experience art, let them choose the medium. Modified schedules can include a lot of real experience/peer tutoring or work experience time. Think about ways to pair children up to help get work done.

Next, let us talk about a dedicated workspace for your child. In education, this is called "Cued for Learning". Just by walking into the school building every day, their brains switch to learning mode. Children recognize the purpose of the building, the classrooms, the posters, the teacher, and their brains will switch to learning mode with no help from them. Setting up a learning workspace will help them settle into the routine of learning much faster and with ease. Setting up a dedicated learning space for each child is important because the minute they enter that space, their brain will automatically switch to learning mode. They have no control over it and teachers rely on it.

The most important focus of a dedicated workspace is to reduce distractions, increase comfort, and provide all materials for learning. This space should be their own. Let them decorate it, bring in comfy pillows, music, favorite objects, a space to store materials, a schedule, notebooks, reading books, and any other thing that will help them get their work done. Make sure that all the items in their workspace are not distracting, i.e. tablets, video games, toys, pets, etc. Learning space should be noise-free, and distraction-free. If you have several children working at the same table, create carrels that they can personalize. Carrels are cardboard, trifold surrounds that give an element of privacy for each student. Schools often use them for testing multiple students at the same time. These increases focus on learning while reducing visual and auditory distractions. Try to keep noise levels to a minimum by turning TVs down, get earbuds for music, etc.

Once you have set up a schedule, post it in their learning space. Use sticky notes, either on their computer or on the wall, to provide websites, passwords, cue cards, multiplication tables, reference cards, Have a magazine holder for notebooks, study guides, extra pencils, etc. that can be shelved when not needed anymore. In other words, the more you organize the space, the easier it is for children to navigate their schoolwork and learning. Make it fun! Use color-coding, cartoons, fun names, fun signs to make the workspace interesting, and engaging for your children. The secret is...all the colors, cartoons and signs remind the children about the learning, procedures, and expectations. They grab attention for a reason.

Remember how you might have set up your office or workspace at your job. You might have had pictures of your kids, your favorite pictures, sayings, plants, fidget toys, etc. That is what you and children will be doing for their school. This is now their workspace. If they need a fidget item great! If they need a picture of their favorite sports team for inspiration, great! This new environment for learning will be more personally theirs than ever before, tailored to their needs. The best part is that for students that need more reminders, they now have the privacy to set up the supports that they need without other students being able to see. Explore, have fun, enjoy creating an environment that works for your child.

2 PROCEDURES

How many interruptions can one person manage a day? 100s in the day. "Teacher, I need the bathroom", Teacher, I need a pencil", "Teacher, where is the notebook?" "Teacher so and so keeps bothering me." In order to decrease the number of interruptions and meet the needs of all students and teachers, Procedures are the way to go and the only cure. Even in the virtual classroom, I use procedures for student responses, use of the microphone, requesting help from the teacher, stepping away, sharing, etc.

The second strategy to begin in any Learning Environment is Procedures. Procedures are a set of actions conducted to maintain consistency with all students and smooth out the daily tasks and operations of the learning environment. These are ways of requesting assistance, completing tasks/assignments, checking grades, handing homework/assignments, requesting bathroom breaks, tissue, extra supplies, and communicating with everyone in the learning environment. Think of Procedures as an operating manual for the Learning Environment for all students. Procedures answers all questions like; How do I get this? How do I go here? When do I get to take a break? What do I do if I break my pencil? What if I do not understand the work? How do I stop so and so from bothering me? Once those questions are answered, most interruptions disappear. If you preload Procedures by establishing them at the beginning, interruptions never occur unless it is something critical.

Procedures also follow comfort levels and preferences. How do you want your children to get your attention other than "Mom, mom, mom, mom, mom, Mom...?" I don't know how many times I heard "Teacher, teacher, teacher, teacher, teacher... Until I fell in love with Procedures. I started small with small problems. If you need a pencil, raise your hand with your pointer finger up. If you need a bathroom break, raise your hand with your thumb across your palm (Letter B in Sign Language). If you need to move out of your seat for any reason, raise your hand with fingers wide and shake. I set up my procedures to account for my distractibility as well. I often got distracted wondering what student A was doing at the pencil sharpener again. Or why student B was in the room library when he was supposed to be in a small group. I also had one classroom procedure where their pockets (the back of pants pockets) remained on the seat until they had my permission to leave it. I did not want students wandering the classroom because it distracted me and other students. I also had a signal where I hold up one finger (means one minute) to ask them to wait if I am supporting another student, talking with another teacher, answering the phone, or completing paperwork for the office.

Students learn the preferences of each teacher they have and adapt to each classroom they are in. There were a few teachers that used different colored sticky notes for signals. Some teachers want students to take care of needs without involving the teacher so their students were able to sharpen pencils, etc. without asking for permission. It really depends on the number of procedures that you need. Creating Procedures is simply **How** you want your children to communicate with you. Do you want them yelling "Mom, mom, mom..." whenever they have a question or need help? Or would a colored sticky note on the top of the computer work? Is there a bell they could ring? At home, children might not need to request a bathroom break but may need help if a sibling is off task and bothering them. How do you want them to handle that? Do you want them to manage it themselves with predetermined procedures or do you want them to let you know so that you can handle it? Think about the biggest interruptions that you experience during the day and that is where a Procedure will cure the problem. How do they let you know they are all done? Do you want them to move on to video games or tablets before you can check their work? Do you want to check their work before they move on to other subjects, or would you rather do it at the end of the day? Procedures are simple sets of actions that communicate results during the school day about all the tasks that need to be completed or managed. One of the best resources for suggestions of Procedures is your children. Ask them how their teacher handled turning in work, checking work, transitioning from one activity to another, free time, etc. Without a doubt, their teacher had a procedure that fit the event.

Once you have established your Procedures, celebrate them. Reward them. Talk about them and how they help everyone. Believe me, when I say, children do not enjoy chaos anymore that most adults do. I had a friend of mine ask me why her son got an upset stomach every day at school. After asking a few questions about the classroom he was in, I realized that he had a brand-new teacher and had been complaining to mom how often the class went off course during the day. This example illustrates that children like and require a certain level of predictability and structure to feel comfortable in the environment and learn. Establishing Procedures will support you and your children in creating a learning environment that will work for everyone.

Design by David Watson

Examples...You might not be aware that your kids have chores at school. They might have an assigned role or just be part of the regular straightening up of the classroom every day. At school, children put books away, pick up the paper on the floor, organize materials, and anything else that promotes personal responsibility for their learning and the classroom family. It teaches them personal responsibility and the responsibility of the unit. They are praised for doing so! They feel good about contributing to the group and take pride in doing it.

Procedures are also how we take care of our materials, our room, our personal items, our classmates, our teachers, etc. So you can have procedures for putting your computer away at the end of the day, picking up all items around your work area, making sure that mom/dad has checked your work before turning off your computer, putting chairs/pillows/tables back in order, taking all snack or lunch leftover items to the kitchen or garbage. They can also the process to sign in online, what websites they are allowed to access, asking permission to use chatting features that are available in most virtual classrooms, using webmail and features, and how to productively wait for your attention. In other words, procedures are the answer to all the reminding that we do as adults to get children to keep things in order. Make a poster, a sticker chart, a progress picture, a point card or anything else that you and your children might think is fun to remember and reward the following procedures.

3 EXPECTATIONS

Am I speaking Greek? These children aren't listening to me! Have you ever noticed, in your child's school classroom, how many posters the teacher has on her/his walls? They have posters, charts, graphs, reminders, rules, and other things that students and teachers forget daily and need to be reminded of are there for them to use. Those posters and charts are filled with Protocols, Procedures, Expectations, and Consequences. These are the governing elements for every classroom. Have you ever visited a classroom where it seems like the teacher does not seem to have control and things seem chaotic? That is a classroom where these 4 steps are not firmly embedded in anyone's mind. Students do not know what to do or what to do next, so they make their own choices, and sometimes not beneficial ones. Teachers will then hop from one crisis to another to get through the academic materials and constantly remind students to get back on task. It becomes a revolving argument between teachers and students to get the work done. It is a power struggle, and no one wins until they let go. Teachers then have no other time to complete all the other tasks that they are required to do and leave the classroom every day feeling exhausted. Sound familiar? When Distance Learning starts for parents, you might feel like you are just running from one fire to another.

Most teachers know that we do not control students, we control the

Learning Environment. If we can set up Expectations and practice those expectations, most students will feel comfortable in the Learning Environment, and feeling comfortable is essential to student's learning. Expectations will look different for you than it will for a classroom, or your neighbors, family, etc. Why? Because it will be unique to you, your children, and your environment. Every classroom has its own personality and every family does too. Not to mention, that what works for one child, will not work for another. I had to construct multiple plans for different students that thought differently, reacted differently, or was motivated differently than the other students. In most classrooms, teachers have class-wide expectations, small group expectations, and sometimes individual expectations for specific students. All of those work together to maintain control of the Learning Environment, not the students. If you think about maintaining the Environment, instead of the student, everything will flow more effectively and efficiently.

Expectations tend to change from classroom to classroom. Why do you ask? Because each teacher has their own level of comfort, pet peeves, and a focus for their classroom. Students will learn the norm for each teacher and adhere to them while in that classroom. For example, I am personally very noise sensitive. My classroom expectations always include "Inside voices" which students knew meant a lower volume than other classes. I had no problem with them quietly talking with other students during class if it doesn't disrupt the class. Some teachers allow no talking at all and still other teachers love cooperative conversations among their students for the entire class. Each of us all has specific ways of doing things. None of it is wrong, it is just individual. You will find some you like, some you do not and some you will change because it did not work out the way you imagined. It is a work in progress.

The set of Expectations is what drives all interaction in the class. The importance cannot be understated, or chaos will reign. This is where students learn what their basic behavior in the Learning Environment must look like to meet the needs of all, including yours. Teachers have multiple tasks in the classroom, so we depend on our students to follow expectations and operate independently so that we can get all our tasks done. Parents that engage in Virtual Education or Homeschooling have other tasks as well. Your children need to be able to complete academic tasks independently for you to manage other children, cook, clean, work, etc. Successful homeschool learning environments can utilize these tools to get multiple children in multiple grade levels through their coursework successfully.

Let us get started. The first thing that you will need to do is to make a list of things you are particularly sensitive to. This list of preferences will help you decide what Expectations you have for your children while they are engaged in learning.

Checklist

o   Too loud
o   Too much movement
o   Too many Interruptions
o   Too much tattling
o   Too much talking
o   Off topic talking
o   Repetitive noises
o   Arguing
o   Negotiation
o   Procrastination
o   Messiness
o   Invasion of others' space
o   Too much teasing

Once you have your list, reduce it by combining some of the similar sensitivities. Make the list as simple as possible so that it can be easily remembered. I incorporated all my sensitivities into just 3 things (called the "Rule of 3").

1. I am Respectful.
2. I am Engaged.
3. I am On Time.

Everyone can remember 3 things easily, all adults and all children. How successful are you at getting your kids to clean their rooms? For myself, it was an ongoing battle of discarded toys, crumpled paper, clothes that could walk themselves to the washer, and unrecognizable items that never saw the garbage can. I started using the Rule of 3 when I sent my own children to clean up their rooms, I used to break it down into 1. Dirty Clothes in the hamper, 2. Toys where they belong, 3. Borrowed items go home (this covers dishes, cups, pillows, etc.). Did it get their rooms completely clean? No, but it was a good starting place and did not overwhelm them at the start. Then I could follow up with "Now that I can see your carpet, it looks like that needs a good clean too." Or "It might look perfect if all your books were on the shelf." The "Rule of 3" can encompass everything that you need them to remember or just the place to start the process. The more you practice the Rule of 3, the more automatic it becomes for everyone. It also takes some dedicated practice when you first start to embed it in memory.

To get started right and firmly embedded the ideas in everyone's mind, at the beginning of the school year, I model what the Expectations "looks like" and "sounds like." Many teachers recommend including pictures of the Expectations behavior to help embed the Expectations in the children's' minds. One teacher took pictures of the students as they completed the Expectations and used those as the pictures for the chart. Way to personalize the chart! Then the class would spend the first couple of days enacting the Expectations. Of course, I made a game out of it with teams and rewards just to get the party started. Once we had practiced for a few days, and I knew my students had it down, I rewarded less often and started doing monthly checks of Expectations. Let us talk a little about how these Expectations are used.

"I am Respectful" means inside volume positive words that include manners like please and thank you in my classroom. It also means being respectful with facial expression, body language, actions, and written/spoken word choices. We practice what being respectful looks like and sounds like the first week of school. It is also a great time to have a dialog about how it feels when others are not respectful to you/me. I found that making a game out of it really helps to make it fun and gives the students opportunities to practice the "I am Respectful". In that first week, every time someone exhibited "I am Respectful" that team got points. If I was busy and did not see the respectful act, the students always let me know what I missed. They want those points. Instead of having a student "tattle" on each other for breaking the rules, they were "tattling" about positive events. What a nice change! (Important to note, I never took away points for negative behavior. I did not want students "tattling" to win.) So, the Expectations game was independent of any other management strategy. At the end of the week, the team with the highest points gets to "cash in" their points for a reward (extra recess, early lunch, extra computer time, etc.). These competitions used to be extremely competitive and I never saw that much considerate and friendly behavior at any other time of the year. Does it wear off? Of course, and occasionally we would have mini competitions that would last for a week or a special occasion just to get them back on track. Did it cost me anything? No. Maybe a little time and flexibility for whatever (non-monetary) reward they chose. Frankly, it was the most effective Learning Environment management tool I ever found and cost nothing to create.

"I am Engaged" means working on tasks independently, not distracting other students in the classroom, completing the assignment completely. Now, engagement can look like quite different things to different people. Some teachers see engagement as any conversation or action that follows the learning goals. They do not mind multiple conversations going on in the class if the conversation is academically related. Others have specific ideas of quiet students working at their computers. You will need to define what engagement looks like for you and then model your Engagement for your children. It might mean, show me work that is done or staying in your own space while working, or eyes on your computer/desk/worksheet. It really depends on what outcomes you want. I can then use the key phrase of "Are you engaged?" when students are having side conversations, talking during instruction time, out of seat/area when they are supposed to be working on a project, etc. The simple phrase reminds them that "I am Engaged" has a set of Expectations that they need to remember. It takes the work out of keeping them focused or on task and it leaves little room for argument or negotiation.

"I am On Time" means not dawdling through every assignment or task, making others wait for you and being prepared for class/tasks when they need to be done. Be on Time can also mean that they follow directions the first time, do not give excuses, or do not try to negotiate a different outcome. This became my "go to" for all transition times (lining up for lunch/recess, library time, computer lab), changes in subjects, classroom tasks like; clean-up, returning materials and handing in assignments. "I am On Time" means do it correctly, quickly, and positively (no grumbling or complaining).

Think of the "Rule of 3" is a way to condense the list of things that you identified as your sensitivities into 3 easily remembered and easy reminders that you can use at any time. If a student is off task or out of their seat, I would quickly ask "Are you engaged?" Or if one of the students was taking his time getting ready for lunch by reorganizing his desk, I would simply remind him by saying "Are you On Time?" Since I have previously modeled and explained those Expectations, students immediately know what I am talking about in 3-4 short words. This set of Expectations become the key phrases that remind them of target actions, reduce arguments about tasks, and generally allow everything in your learning environment to move fluently through the day.

Design by Renee Walls

Your set of Expectations does not need to be long or cover every contingency. It needs to cover the basic behaviors that you will expect from your children during their learning time. Do you expect them to talk respectfully to others? Do you expect them to keep hands and feet to self? Do you expect them to respect other people's property? Do you expect them to respond appropriately when you give them a direction? Do you expect them to work independently? What it does not include is emotions, thoughts, or attitudes. Children have a right to those. What it does include is the basic set of Expected Norms for the Learning Environment. Decide what you think is most important and plan for that.

Once you have your list and your keywords, create some easy reminders. I used posters, but many teachers had creative ways of displaying their Expectations. Framed pictures with artwork was one fun way. Collages, wall art, book covers, and stamped pencils/sticky notes were some of the other creative ways of reminding children. Make your Expectations your own. Create a game to go along with them. Create a progress sticker chart. Create a system for tracking the expectations that will allow you to lengthen the time between rewarding that behavior and begin to instill the idea that Expectations is an everyday activity.

4 MANAGING BEHAVIOR

Why does my house seem like a zoo and I am the lion tamer?!!! While fielding phone calls from parents at the onset of distance learning, some things were going well but I often heard two concerns repeatedly. "My child is refusing to do the work" and "I'm tired of the tantrums." When you first begin distance learning and everyone is trying on new hats, it can be really frustrating especially when everyone feels overwhelmed and lost. Even though I already work in a virtual school, when schools shut down nationwide many of my parents complained about their children refusing to work. Their children were upset that our school was not closed, and they still had work when all the neighbor children were outside playing. Finding incentives for children is sometimes hard when they perceive that "it's not fair". We are going to talk about how to counteract some of the behaviors that you might see when children are frustrated or lost.

Managing behavior is a system too. I have enjoyed learning so many different theories and matrixes to understand what consequences to use and what was appropriate for each level of behavior. It is a balancing act to be sure. When does the behavior need Expectations reminders? When does the situation need Procedure/Protocols reminders? What is the system of evaluating behavior to know which method to use? The first question you need to ask is "What is the behavior that you are trying to change?" If it is following Expectations, then reminders are all that you need. If it is following Procedures, reminders are all that you need. If it is following Protocols, getting work done, completing assignments, copying other work, etc. then you might need to use some more intensive strategies to help children remember the appropriate behavior. Your rewards charts at home may look a little different than mine. You need to focus on the behaviors that you have the most problems with and then reward the opposite (target) behavior. Do you have problems with children touching other children (hands and feet to self), pestering other children (zero voice during work time), trying to get attention (raise your hand and wait), bathroom breaks every 30 minutes, tattling, breathing noisily, tapping pencils/feet non-stop, making faces, and so much more? How do you manage to teach you wonder? Yep it is hard! The minute that those little bodies get bored or overwhelmed, all kinds of responses pop up.

Consequences fall into two different categories (rewards and discipline) and two different levels (mild and serious). Rewards are pre-determined "paychecks" that children receive for doing what is expected or defined. Good grades are a reward. Getting work done early is a reward. Getting a high five is a reward. Feeling good about what they did is a reward. We all get rewarded every day. Rewards are delivered according to the continuum of smallest to largest. The small rewards are given for behavior that should be automatic but are not yet. Big rewards are given for behavior that has long range consequences and could be considered "life skills".

The same is true of discipline. Small disciplines are ways of reminding children what they should be doing. Gentle reminders that they might be off track or forgetting the expectations. More serious or chronic behavior requires more intentional discipline. But remember what I promised you in the first couple of chapters, if you practice learning environment management, you will not need to utilize discipline very often or ever. The level of severity of the behavior starts with mild and ends with severe. Behaviors that occur in the mild level are behaviors like not following protocols, procedures, or expectations. These are most like misdemeanors. They break the law but do not really harm anyone. Consequences are the tickets that you get for not following the rules. Most people will remember to wear their seatbelts after one ticket. These are reminders to be safe and responsible. More serious behaviors are actions that can cause harm, harm to self, harm to others or to property. You can break down most all behavior into those two levels.

Rewards

The first and most powerful consequence is rewards. If you think about it for a minute, we (adults) are rewarded for behavior every day. If you work, you get a paycheck. If you cook, you get a meal. If you build, you get a house. Right! As adults, we understand the concept of delayed gratification. In other words, our paycheck does not arrive every day. We must accumulate enough worked hours to get a solid paycheck. Younger children and some teenagers have not yet realized the concept of "banking" what we do for the "payday" later. They require "instant" rewards. And those instant rewards are what builds the motivation to keep going even when the work seems hard. Who does not love a treat now and again? Now do not go thinking that you have to break the bank here to provide rewards for your children/students.

Rewards are not always big. Sometimes it is simply acknowledgement of what they did or how well they did. You would be surprised how many students work for just a smile. Or a sticker on a chart. Or a break. Or a treat, Or time with friends. Or time with mom/dad, etc., etc. The list is long because every student that I created a menu of rewards for had different items on the menu than the next student. Each child can construct a menu of rewards just for them. Mom/Dad you do not even need to be the one to do it. However, you need to be the one to approve it because you are the one that will be providing it.

Think of managing behavior as a ladder. Rewards for little things, like following classroom expectations, gets little rewards. This is like understanding that we drive on the right side of the road to be safe and keep other people safe. There is no reward for driving on the right side of the road other than arriving alive and not hurting anyone else. That is the level of classroom expectations. Little rewards can be spaced out over hours, days, and weeks for bigger rewards. If you follow classroom expectations for a month, you get a star student award. If you drive on the right side of the road and do not hurt anyone else, insurance costs will go down. Some behaviors should be expected and not rewarded at the higher level because it teaches that we are all members of the same society. These behaviors are what is best for all of us. It is teaching the idea of citizenry and responsibility to society.

The initial and most important reward I would like to talk about is Praise - Highly underrated as a management technique! Teachers are required to have a 4:1 ratio of positive to negative comments for every minute during class time. We are observed and graded on it during every evaluation cycle. Positive comments are things like: "Thanks for hanging up your backpack," "Thanks for sitting in your seat," "Thanks for eyes on teacher," etc. From the moment that your child enters the building, they are constantly told what little "Rockstars" they are for doing the right thing. Things like; standing in line, hands to yourself, putting things in the garbage, cleaning up their food area, getting their work done, sitting quietly, paying attention, working well with others, using the right words, etc. Do not underestimate how powerful one complement can be to get the whole class doing what they should. Children all want to be part of that praise because children love praise. Just as we do.

The second type of reward is tangibles. Another favorite for all of us. Believe when I say, children will work hard for small rewards, like praise, smiles, and high fives for the small stuff. But they will work even more for mini slinkies, fun erasers, pencil toppers, rulers, slime, stretchy toy things that they throw at walls, tiny furry stars, edibles (doesn't always need to be candy), and other small items. My favorite place to shop for small rewards was the dollar stores and the party shops. Anything that will fit into a treasure box will work. It works well with younger children, but I was surprised how many of my middle school students loved it too. Obviously, high school students are motivated by other things but a lot of those things are cost free as well like tickets they can save for extra TV time, reduced chores, time with friends, social online time are some of the best motivators for them. When I was at the high school, my best reward was that I would stop instructing 5 mins before the bell so that they could visit with other students. Worked like a charm and we got so much work done because they just wanted to talk with their classmates for 5 minutes. All children and teens love to practice socializing. Teens are in the developmental stage where socializing is critical in supporting their emerging adulthood.

So, as you are setting up the reward system, Littles might have one reward, Middles might have another, and the Upper grades will have something entirely different. Think about what your kids really love to do; time on tablets, video games, phone calls or social interactions, time with Mom/Dad individually, creative projects, playtime, etc. The targeted rewards are key to a successful rewards program because it reinforces the behavior you want and the reward they want. Rewards do not have to be tangible in nature either. Quality time is a big reinforcement. While you are making your reward chart, you can also build a menu of reward options that your kids choose from when they earn a reward. Have your children fill out a card of things they would like to receive as a reward, review them to make sure you are comfortable with them and then post them on the fridge. You will achieve better control of your class by always providing choices that support their need for empowerment.

Consequences

On the opposite side of reward is discipline. All learning environments must address times when children are not doing what they should. In the traditional system, you have probably received a copy of the discipline policy from your local school district. What happens when children do not do what you want them to do? What are the consequences? Is the non-compliance minor or major? How long should the discipline last? Rule of thumb, consequences must fit the crime. Schools have divided discipline into categories and levels for many years to address the more serious behaviors. Check out the discipline policy for your district online to get a sense of what the structure should be. It is important to remember the main goal of discipline is to support the child in gaining control of themselves and make better decisions.

For mild behaviors (not harmful), Learning Environment transgressions are usually handled with error correction, re-direction or seclusion which is "Time Out" or "Seat Away" in order to gain control of themself. This allows them to self-regulate. Then the child regains control and thinks about the expectations. Before I use these strategies though, I would start with my expectations. "Are you on time?" "Are you engaged?" "Are you respectful?" If those reminders did not work, then my go-tos were simple and easy for the students and myself to remember.

1. Re-phrase or Re-do
2. Try that again
3. Seat Away in class, also known as Time Out, Regrouping, Thinking, or Peace chair
4. Seat Away in hallway
5. Call to parent to inform of possible further action
6. Office referral

Truthfully, I rarely got past number 3. Most all students make mistakes and given the opportunity to correct them, they will. When we got to number 4-6, another level of consequences kicked in. That level may require some kind of reparation (extra chores, fixing what you destroyed, making a new one, apologizing, or seclusion/grounded, etc.). Dividing your system of discipline into levels will really help in understanding how to address the type of behavior you are dealing with and what to do about it. Remember, shaming, blaming or humiliation really do not motivate change and can make the behavior more resistant to change. Empowering your child to make appropriate choices is a much stronger motivational tool.

Consequences

1. Rephrase/Redo

2. Try it again

3. Think Chair

4. Time Away

Designed by Laura Reyes

Level one infractions can be handled with the first 3 responses. "Rephrase-Redo" gives the child the opportunity to do it the right way and receive praise for it (I also praise for a redo). It falls under the category of error correction. It also gives them the practice of what it feels like when they do it correctly. "Try that again" is an opportunity to make the right choice. This is usually used when the child is struggling with emotions and not making great choices. "Try that again" allows them to demonstrate that they can make good choices and I praise them for a good choice. Seat Away in class is when the child is removed from reinforcements and is actively practicing a method to regain control (make a small poster card with steps as a reminder). This means they can see and hear all that is going on but are removed from interactions, including interactions with the other children (social reinforcement) while they are in Seat Away. (It is important to note that the understanding of Time Out/Seat Away is 1 min for every year of age, ex. 3 years old is 3 minutes.) Once they are in control of themselves and ready to participate, I praise them for returning to what they should be doing. There are many self-management/calm down techniques available online for children and I encourage you to explore them to find one that fits your family. If these consequences do not work, then move on to level two.

Level two is reserved for chronic behaviors that level one consequences are not changing. However, it is also the starting place for a sudden occurrence of behaviors that are harmful or more serious than not following protocols, procedures, or expectations. (Important to note, extremely aggressive, self-injurious, suicidal, or sexual behavior is not included in this level. Those behaviors should be addressed by a professional.) Serious behaviors may be throwing something at another child, stealing, naughty words, tearing things up, constant interruptions, bothering another child, knocking things over, repeatedly not following directions, and direct disobedience to name a few. Even with serious behaviors, the goal is still to allow the child to gain control and then make the appropriate choice. They may need some time away from all distractions to do that and that is why it is called seclusion. Some examples might be: Take 5 mins in your room to get your anger under control, take 5 mins to find the answer to why you need to talk to your sister respectfully. Children can leave seclusion when they are calm, and they have the answer to how to amend their behavior.

So now let us talk about the meltdowns, and/or tantrums. They can look very much alike but quite different. You need to look at the source of the problem before deciding how to deal with it. Emotional meltdowns (and we have all had them, remember the faculty bathroom) come from an emotional place of feeling overwhelmed, frustrated, grief, and loss. Although on the surface this looks like a behavior, it is really a strong visceral reaction to the situation. When anyone, child, or adult, is in the middle of a "melt-down" they are in the middle of an emotional crisis. So, let us talk about how to handle an emotional crisis. I have had a lot of conversations with parents about meltdowns now. Both students and parents are melting down. Some advice and I do not mean to offend. Let it be! You and your student are in a process. There will be melt-downs! The best response is to not react to the melt-down. It will only escalate the crisis. Give them a pillow, walk away, and allow them to regain some self-control before trying to talk it out. Allow yourself to gain control before trying to help them manage their behavior. They are grieving! They are grieving every relationship that they had at school, the lunch ladies, playground monitor, their teachers, friends, and every other person at school that told them how wonderful they were every day at school. And all those people at school are grieving the relationship they had with your child. As are you as the parent, grieving the loss of your independence, privacy, routines, etc. It is a trigger for you and for them. You both need compassion in this moment.

In comparison to "melt-downs", tantrums have a different source than an emotional crisis. Tantrums can be a behavior designed to get something or avoid something. Think about times when a child that you know might have had a tantrum. Was it to get a popsicle? Or a toy? Or a video game? Or an item that you did not want them to have at the that moment? OR was it to get out of going to bed? Or getting homework done? Mowing the grass? Or doing their schoolwork? These types of behaviors are a form of communication if the child does not have sufficient vocabulary to describe what they want or are feeling in the moment. However, it can also be a reinforced behavior to control their environment. It is important to understand why the behavior is occurring before you address it. (Note - extremely aggressive, self-injurious, suicidal, or sexual behavior are not included in this description)

The first step responds to the main goal of consequences for tantrums which is to allow the child to regain control of their behavior and emotions in a space where it does not disturb anyone else or cause harm. Unless the behavior is harmful, try not to react to the tantrum other than to say, "Once you are in control of yourself, then we can talk", then walk away. Walk far enough away to not engage in the behavior but close enough to still be able to monitor them for harmful behavior. Once they have regained control of themselves, then you can address the potential outcomes. An appropriate response to "get something" would be to make the something conditional being earned. Is there something they could do to "earn" the item that they want? An appropriate response to "avoid something" would be to allow them the choice of when they need to complete it. I often gave the students a binary (two) choice format to choose from. If you want a popsicle, you can clean your room or walk the dog. If you do not want to work on math now, then we can work on math before dinner or after dinner today. Children love to have choices too. One of the best pieces of advice that I received from another parent was to always make sure that the choice options were always something I was comfortable with too. Developing human beings have an innate ability to choose the one you may not want them to choose. Remember that tantrums are typical with younger children. Most children will not be having a tantrum when they are 23 years old and do not want to go to work.

As you move through consequences, remember that the goal of consequences is to allow them to gain control of themselves, teach the child appropriate behaviors, and provide ways to receive the rewards of appropriate actions. Just like we, ourselves, fail and then try again, children need to be able to correct mistakes gracefully and then enjoy the moments of success.

5 EDUCATIONALLY RELEVANT ACTIVITIES

Sometimes I think this day will never end! You might wonder what educationally relevant activities means or where the phrase came from. Educationally relevant activities are a description that most states have in their education policy that specifies what occurs during the 6.5 hours of the school day. It is the standard that decides whether we can count that child as attending school for an entire school day. This attendance policy is what determines how many children were served that day and for how long. Attendance calculations are what determines school budgets for operation based on the number of students attending school. Because distance learning allows for the ability of students to complete their work in under 6.5 hours, the remainder of the time must be spent in educationally relevant activities suggested by teachers or determined by parents according to state educational policies. I must point out, though, that these activities do not replace the core curriculum coursework. It is simply what the rest of the day should look like.

Educationally Relevant Activities is really a bonus to all learning coordinators (parents and teachers). This might be what is called "teachable moments", but it really goes beyond that. It is really where education and academic content meets real life. Where do we use all the things, we learned in school every day? Where do we use Math? Where do we use Social Studies? Where do we use Science? Educationally Relevant Activities are anything we might do where we use the knowledge and skills that we learned in school. Just for an example, cooking uses Math (fractions, measurement) and Science (combining elements and chemical reactions). What happens when heat is applied? Or cooling? How is the product beneficial to the consumer (health class)? What is the nutritional value of the product? How do you write a recipe (Language Arts)? Are you going shopping? Have your children calculate the cost of things in the basket.

They can compare the cost of different brands. For older children, they can research how that item was produced, branding, effects of advertising, etc. Basically, you can turn most daily activities into an educationally relevant activity without too much effort.

Even the time spent playing with toys can be defined as learning time. Building with Legos is a real application of sorting by size, color, or type. Planning or sequencing skills are used to build Lego structures. Legos can be used to practice measuring area or perimeter (Math). Building a project birdhouse uses Math, Science and Critical Thinking Skills. If your child likes video games, there are so many online educational games that are made in video game formats. They can play a video game and learn Math, Science, Typing, Reading, and Writing. Is watching TV a favorite pastime? Then check out the educational videos and shows online. They can watch animal videos, history videos, social studies, current events, and science shows (most cartoons do not count).

So, we can probably find that most daily activities, including chores, have some base knowledge or skill that we acquired in school. All these activities are real applications of school content and are educationally relevant activities. Now you are following State and Local Educational Policies.

CONCLUSION

My idea of writing this book came from the many tearful phone calls and overwhelming frustration parents were feeling during this onset of Distance Learning. It was not most parents' first choice and they were immediately overwhelmed with the volume of work and activities that their children are required to do on an average day at school. Yes, school days are busy and hectic and filled with hours of learning, activities, responsibilities, and structure. But the school day is also filled with laughter, excitement and caring. Learning should be fun. That was always my intent in my class every day. Make this adventure fun for you and your children. These strategies are ways to help you deal with the immense number of tasks required in education but that does not mean that these tasks cannot be fun. Make it your own! It is your Learning Environment. If your children are completing their coursework and learning, it does not mean that you cannot have a lot of fun doing it. You do not have to do it the way the teachers did it in your children's school. As a matter of fact, you cannot. So, create a system that works for you. Children respond to humor in learning. Things that are fun are more easily remembered than things that are hard. That is why the Alphabet Song is so popular. It is why teachers make a card game out of sight words. Think back to your time in school, chances are you remember the fun teachers first. It is ok to be goofy. It is ok to be a clown. It is ok to be yourself. I do it every day in teaching and most of my students love it. Just do not get me sidetracked by asking me about the Galapagos Turtles. That was Benjamin's favorite way to get me off task so that we did not have to do Spelling.

If you enjoyed this book, please leave a review on Amazon :)! Watch for the release of my next book that explain the difference between the "can't" or the "won't".

Thanks,   and   remember   to   just   breathe!

THANKS TO ALL OF YOU

I raised three amazing and challenging children of my own while I was attending classes to complete my degrees. I spent many years reading all kinds of books about parenting and my children's' needs while being a single parent. Much of that knowledge and experience served me well as an educator. Single motherhood is an absolute challenge all of its own and without the support of my children and many dear friends, I would not have made it to where I am today or have completed the courses and learning that have helped me to become the teacher that I am. Thank you to all of you that were my support and believed that I could do this, my children, my friends, my family and my husband!

SOME ONLINE RESOURCES

Note: Here are just a few resources. The best way to find what you need is to search it on the web browser of your choice. Always make sure to put the word "free" or "printable" in front of your search words.

Poster My Wall - Customize and download for free for personal use. https://www.postermywall.com/index.php/posters/search?s=classroom%20rules

Stickers and Charts - Print free progress charts for children https://www.stickersandcharts.com/

More Free Sticker Charts - Free charts and some low cost charts https://www.teacherspayteachers.com/Browse/Search:free%20sticker%20charts

https://www.twinkl.com/resource/t-m-691-reward-sticker-chart-stars

Stickers - You can buy on Amazon, Oriental Trading Company and other school supply stores. Usually 500-100 stickers for under $10 dollars. https://www.amazon.com/s?k=stickers+for+kids&ref=nb_sb_noss

https://www.orientaltrading.com/teaching-supplies-and-stationery/

Conscience Discipline - Resources and tips for management https://consciousdiscipline.com/free-resources/discipline-tips/

LD at School - Behavior management resources https://www.ldatschool.ca/behaviour-managementlds/

ABOUT THE AUTHOR

Susan Pearl-Weese is known for being passionate in her advocacy for Special Education students during her 21 years of teaching Special Education to elementary, middle, and high school students. She has worked with students that have mild challenges to very severe challenges both academically and behaviorally. She served as Director of Special Education to an online charter academy for over 4 years where she became an advocate for parents that were learning how to navigate the Learning Environment and virtual education for the first time. From the time that she became a teacher, she continued her education to increase her knowledge and skills in the areas of Mild/Moderate Special Education, Severe Special Education, English as a Second Language and as a Reading Specialist. She also completed a Master Program for Administrative Supervision. She has experience in traditional physical site schools for over 15 years and virtual education experience for 6 years. The transition to Virtual Education the opportunity for her to support parents as they step into the arena of creating an environment where their children can learn. Her ongoing conversations with many student's parents, hearing their frustrations, anxieties and successes led her to write this book to further support student success.